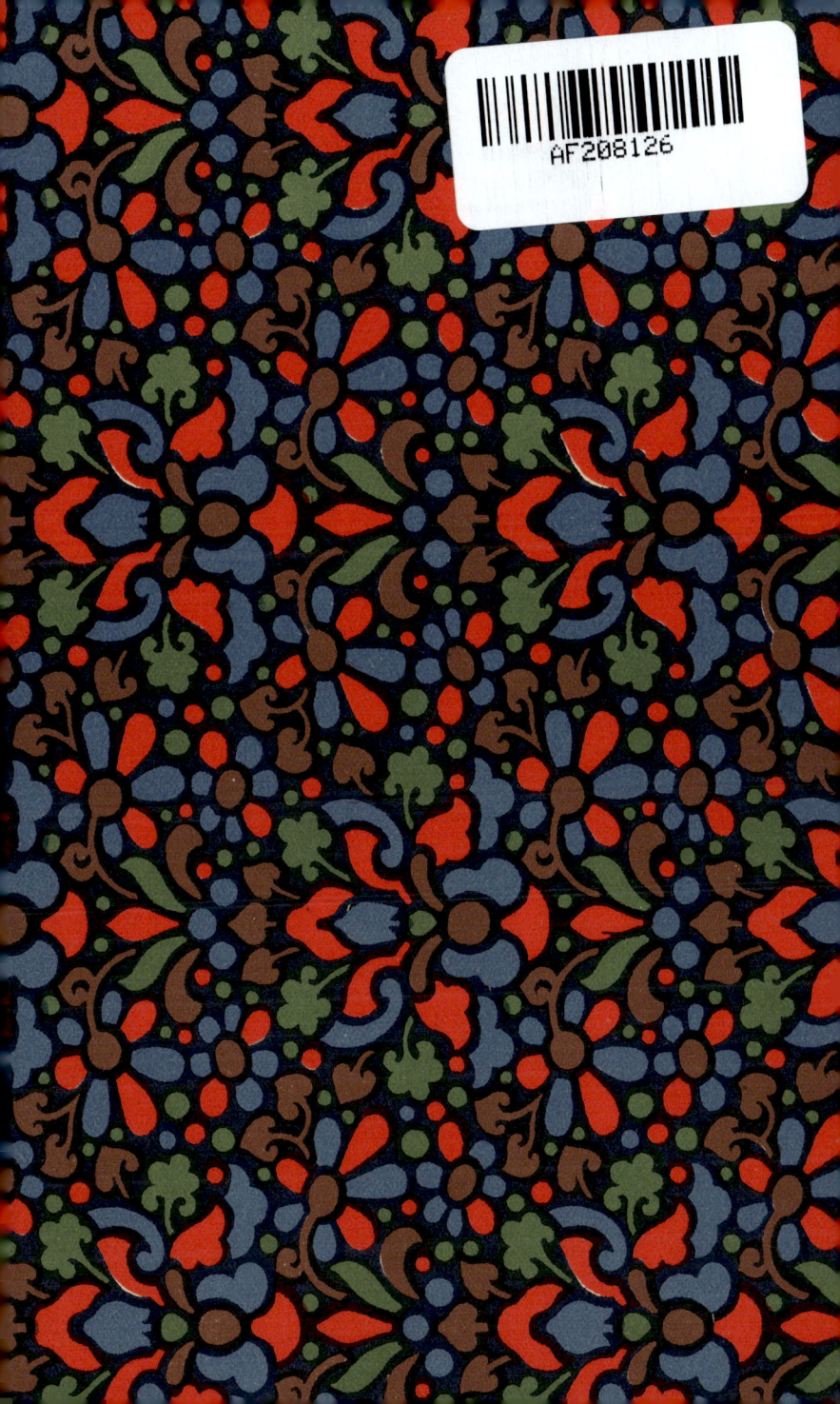

Bea Schlingelhoff

THE CROOKED

Typefaces for Baseless Rumors

366 capping phrases used for kōan practice

2

THE CROOKED
Typefaces for Baseless Rumors

366 capping phrases used for kōan practice.

Capping phrases are different than kōans.

A kōan is a narration, dialogue, story or statement, using contradictions and riddles often ending with or including a question, supplemented with commentaries, and capping phrases. In the Rinzai sect of Zen Buddhism or in Chan Buddhism a kōan is used both as an object of meditation and as an expression of enlightenment. Its rhetoric is often considered anti-intellectual.

The capping phrase or capping verse of a kōan (in Japanese Jakugo, 着語, "language used when writing letters"), or agyo (下語, "baseless rumor") can be a summary or an accepted proof of the solution of the kōan riddle, but never the solution itself. It is often deprived from quotations from Chinese poetry. According to Victor Sōgen Hori, the use of capping phrases was developed from classical Chinese "literary games" used during the Song dynasty (AD 960–1270).

Some schools practice "observing the phrase," which refers to studying one kōan throughout one's lifetime, however there are many different kōan curricula that have diverse classifications and vary in emphasis or even intend.

Example for a kōan and its capping phrase (kōan by Hakuin Ekaku):

The Sound Of One Hand Clapping

The master of Kennin temple was Mokurai, Silent Thunder. He had a little protégé named Toyo who was only twelve years old. Toyo saw the older disciples visit the master's room each morning and evening to receive instruction in sanzen or personal guidance in which they were given kōans to stop mind-wandering. Toyo wished to do sanzen also. "Wait for a while," said Mokurai. "You are too young." But the child insisted, so the teacher finally consented.

In the evening little Toyo went at the proper time to the threshold of Mokurai's sanzen room. He struck the gong to announce his presence, bowed respectfully three times outside the door, and went to sit in front of the master in gracious silence. "You can hear the sound of two hands when they clap together," said Mokurai. "Now show me the sound of one hand."

Toyo bowed and went to his room to consider this problem. From his window he could hear the music of the geishas. "Ah, I have it!" he proclaimed.

The next evening, when his teacher asked him to illustrate the sound of one hand, Toyo began to play the music of the geishas. "No, no," said Mokurai. "That will never do. That is not the sound of one hand. You haven't gotten it at all." Thinking that such music might interrupt, Toyo moved his abode to a quiet place. He meditated again. "What can the sound of one hand be?" He happened to hear some water dripping. "I have it," Toyo thought. When he next appeared in front of his teacher, he imitated dripping water. "What is that?" asked Mokurai. "That is the sound of dripping water, but not the sound of one hand. Try again." In vain Toyo meditated to hear the sound of one hand. He heard the sighing of the wind. But the sound was rejected. He heard the cry of an owl. This was also refused. The sound of one hand was not the locusts either. It has been over ten times, that Toyo had visited Mokurai with different sounds. All were wrong. For almost a year he pondered what the sound of one hand might be.

At last, Toyo reached true meditation and transcended all sounds. "I could collect no more," he explained later, "so I reached the soundless sound." Toyo had realized the sound of one hand.

Capping phrase for this kōan:

隻手声あり、その声を聞け

Two hands clap and there is a sound.
What is the sound of one hand?

For an extended collection of capping phrases, please refer to *Zen Sand. The Book of Capping Phrases for Kōan Practice* by Victor Sōgen Hori, University of Hawai'i Press, Honolulu, 2003. Most capping phrases in this book have been chosen from this source.

Further readings may include *The Zen Koan* by Isshu Miura and Ruth Fuller Sasaki, Harcourt, Brace & World, San Diego, 1965.

8

10

Easy to
call
hard to
send
away

12

EASY
TO
CALL
HARD
TO
SEND
AWAY

EASY TO
CALL

HARD TO
SEND
AWAY

Saying "fire" won't burn your mouth; 17
saying "water" won't drown you.

follow the tides and ride the waves.

Like a shooting spark, like a flash of lightening.

One encounter: once and for all.

24

Bow and withdraw. 25

THE SCARECROW
KEEPS STANDING
HOLDING A BOW
AND ARROW
EVEN AFTER THE
HARVEST IS OVER.

the scarecrow
keeps standing

holding a bow
and arrow

even after the
harvest is over.

A piece of dust in the eye: 31
Illusory flowers dance wildly.

Buying high,

selling

low.

An inch of tortoise hair
weighs seven pounds.

Seven times
take in,
eight times
let go.

Seven times
Take in
eight times
let go.

40

Not knowing is the most intimate.

Do not harp on things that are finished.

44

One who knows well, must act well. 45

46

A team of horses can't catch a word once uttered. 47

One moon shows in every pool;
in every pool the one moon.

50

Speaking without speaking,
knowing without knowing.

52

Not this, not this, not this.

One lamp, ten thousand lamps,
lamp after lamp without end.

56

Water does not wash water;
gold is not changed into gold.

58

THIS
ERROR,
that
error.

60

Words depleted; reason spent. 61

one thousand acts, ten thousand impulses moving all at once.

64

One thousand
acts,
ten thousand
impulses
moving all
at once.

Don't
blame
the
past.

DON'T

BLAME

THE

PAST.

Don't blame the past.

Not yet! Not at all. Never.

I do not need even one thing, 75
much less two or three.

76

Thunder rolls once: a clear wind rises. 77

Store the whole world in a grain of millet!
Boil mountains and rivers in a two-quart pot.

Blue mountains after rainfall—much bluer.

Don't rehash what's already done.

A word once spoken can't be caught by rapid horses.

Appearing like spirits and vanishing like ghosts. 87

WHATEVER
YOU TOUCH
IS
REFRESHING.

Stripped of all personal possessions. 91

92

Forget
before, lose
track
after.

Add where
there's lots,
reduce
where
there's
little.

Love both
host and
guest.

I have no comment.

I have no comment.

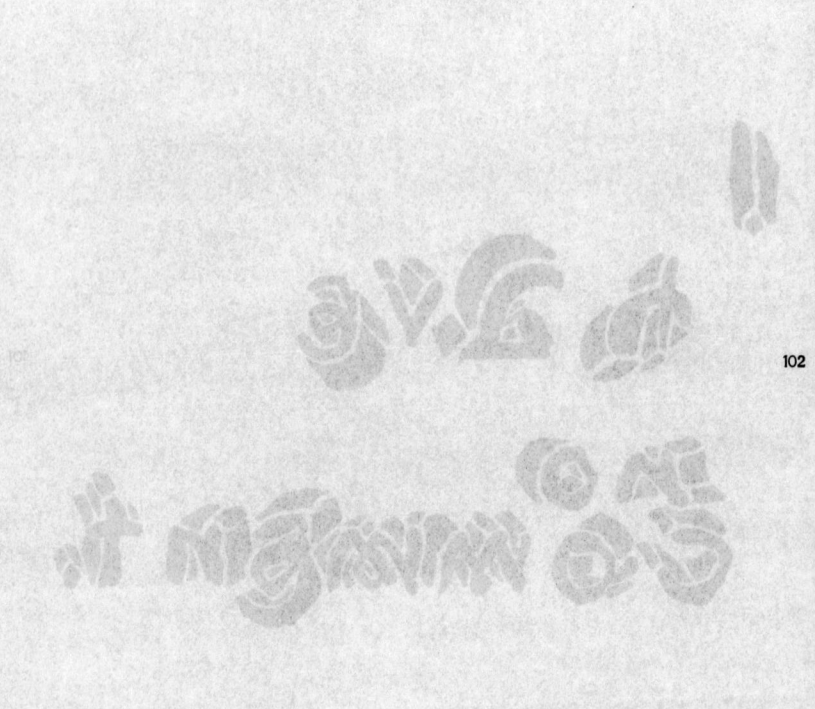

I HAVE
NO
COMMENT.

103

For a thousand ages, no answer.

106

Explained it away. 107

Spotless, transparent.

Heart exposed, naked and red. 111

It is forbidden to tell all. 113

Unsold goods a thousand years old.

There is illumination, there is action.

Much too meticulous.

Face to face, a thousand miles away. 121

The great earth has no outside. 123

As it is right now.

**When you are face to face,
it's hard to hide.**

A drop of water becomes a bead of ice. 129

In the mirror of heaven there is no private self. 131

Goes into mud, goes into water.

As one grows old the heart grows lonely. 135

Take care of yourself on the way.

mind
and
things
are
both
forgotten.

mind

and ~~past~~

things

are both

forgott

en.

mind

and

things

are

born

forgotten.

143

MI ND
AN D
TH IN GS
AR E
BO TH
FO RG OT TEN!

145

In what sense is it far away? 147

MILD AS A CLEAN BREEZE

what is
this before
your very
eyes?

Why in such an awful hurry? 153

Naturally and without effort.

Grip and hold firm, release and let go.

Fire is hot, water is cold. 159

Beat the signal drum, get everyone to help.

There is no explanation.

164

True person without rank.

That's great! That's awful!

The post
the latern.

Blue, yellow,
red, white
black.

171

Totally in action, nothing hidden.

What place cannot be called a place of honor?

Unborn, undying. 177

Close your mouth and say one word.

gET ThE
qEST

get the
question clear
and you are
already close
to the answer.

A worm
cut into
two—
which half
is the true
worm?

IT IS INCONVENIENT FOR ME.

185

To know and yet to enquire is politeness. 187

FIRE DOES NOT DRY, WATER DOES NOT WET.

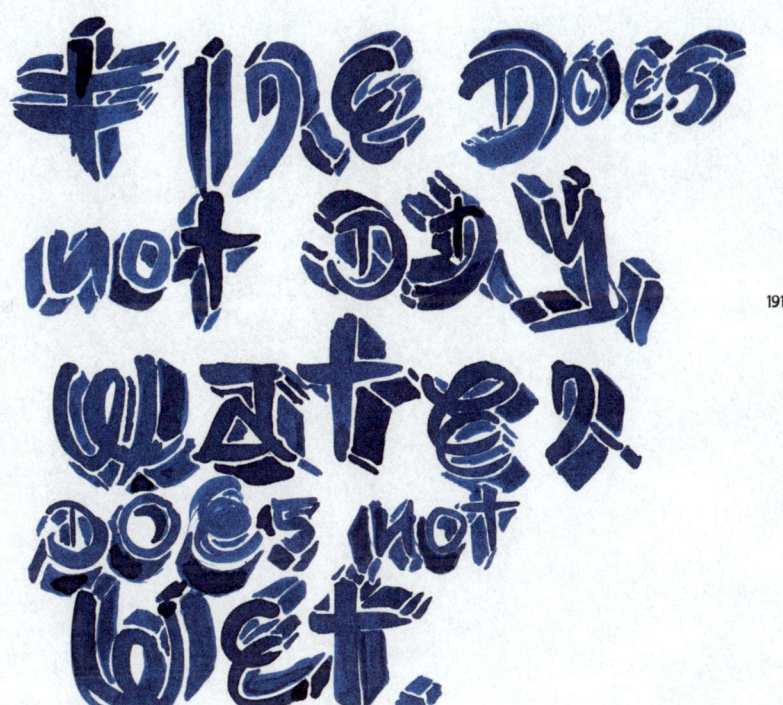

Fire does not dry water does not wet.

FIRE DOES NOT DRY WATER DOES NOT WET.

who would keep you in the dark?

who would keep you in the dark?

197

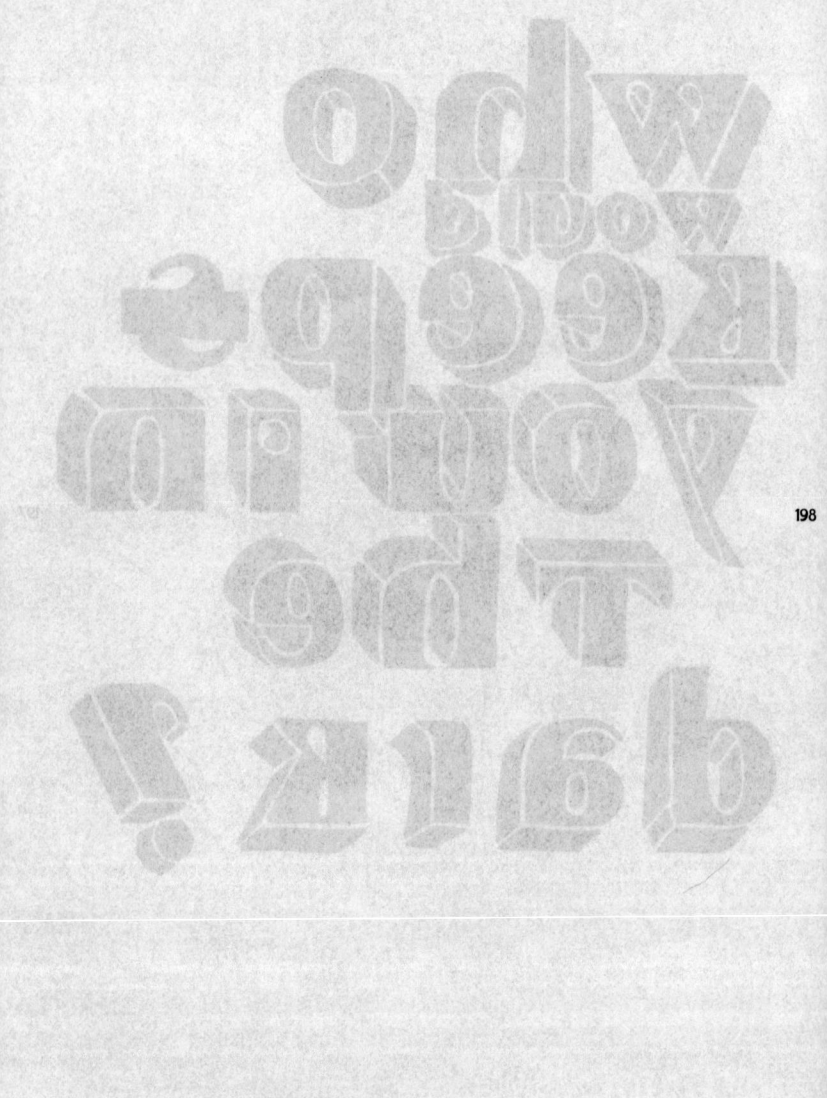

who would keep you in the dark?

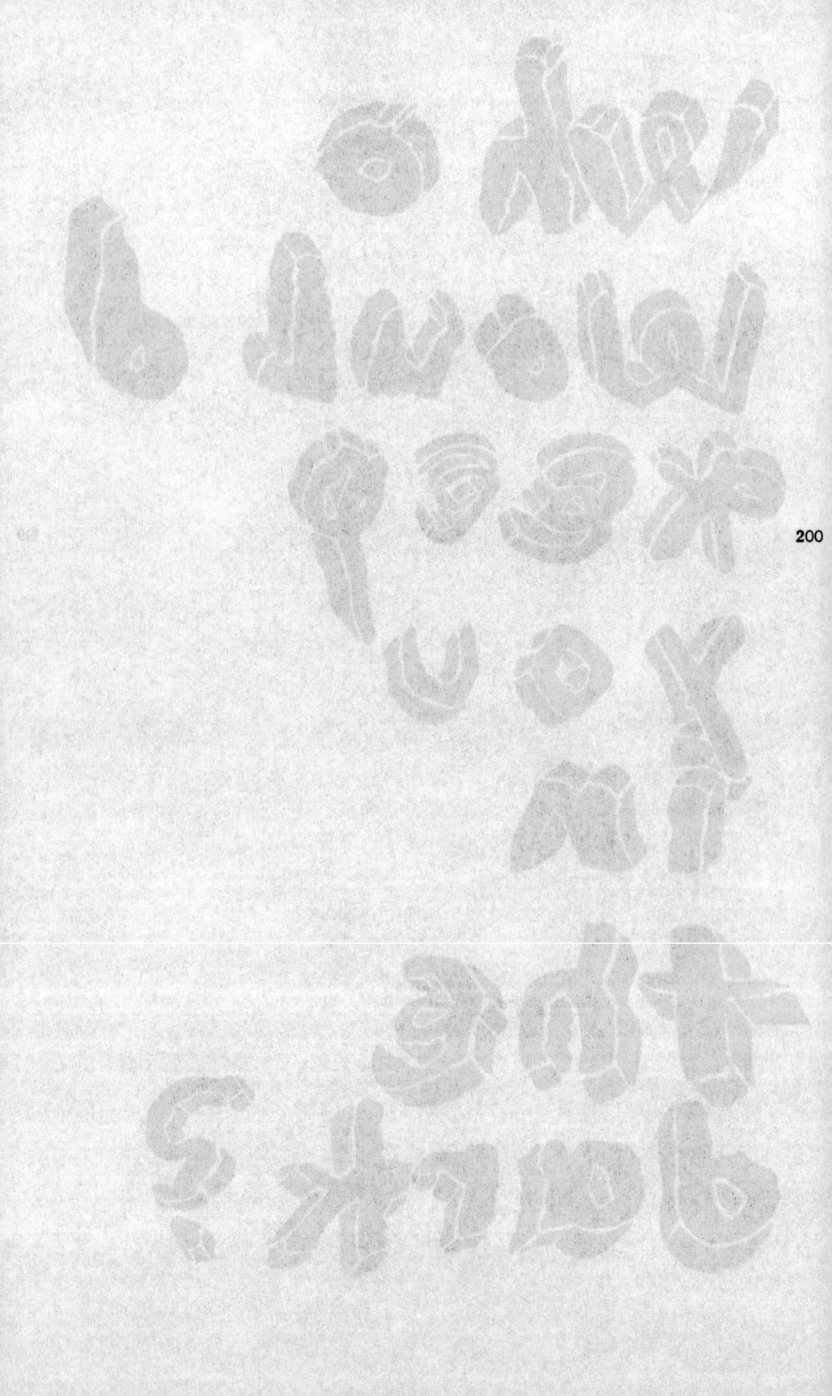

A person in sorrow knows the night is long.

Just before it rains, the mountains look closer. 203

Stone statues whisper to each other.

The wild grasses have never been cut.

A word of confession.

209

210

Fundamentally there is not one thing.

If you slap the water,
you hurt the heads of the fish.

Above, below, and in the four directions,
no rivals.

Falling flowers, flowing waters, limitless, vast. 217

**Seeing without seeing,
hearing without hearing.**

Today there is, tomorrow there isn't.

A long thing is long, a short thing is short.

The flower in the garden, is it alive or dead?

226

Mountains are mountains, rivers are rivers.

Think not good, think not evil.

Pine needles are not straight,
thorns are not curved.

one,

of a half,

of ten

million.

One who
takes
careful
aim
does not
hit the
target.

235

One who takes careful aim does not hit the target.

For evil words that wound a person, 239
resentment never fades.

240

THE
TONGUE
HAS
NO
BONES

~~THE TONGUE~~

~~the tongue~~

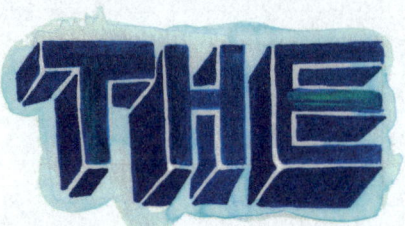

THE TONGUE HAS NO BONES

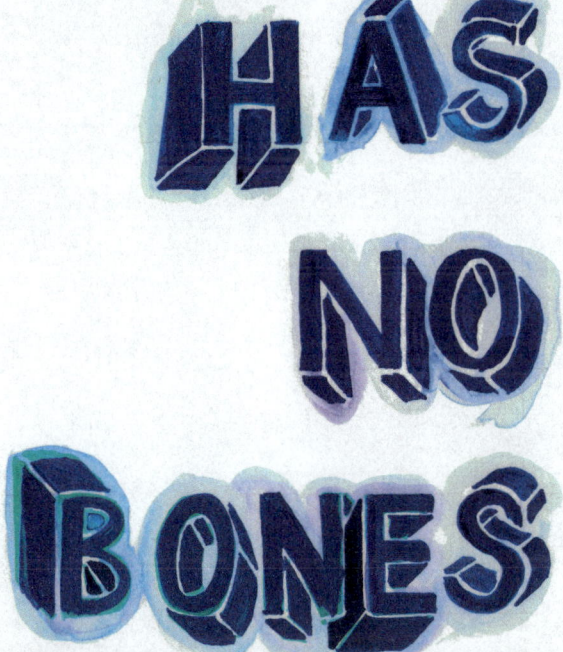

THE TONGUE HAS NO BONES

The tongue has no bones.

The tongue has no bones

One rain wets everything,
covering the entire world.

Wind and dew 251
and the fresh scent of chrysanthemums.

Up in the trees, the carp opens wide its mouth and laughs.

Green mountains after rain,
the green is even greener.

How can a sparrow know
the aspiration of a wild swan?

258

Yesterday it rained, today it's clear. 259

All your bones and joints are made of gold.

At the busy intersection, a worn-out sandal. 263

[redacted]

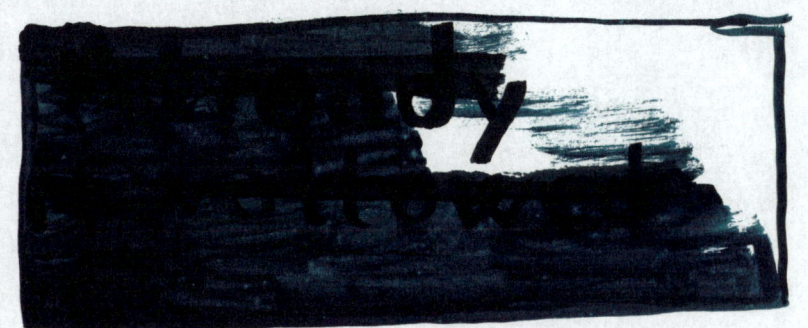

I AM NOT KEEPING ANYTHING FROM YOU.

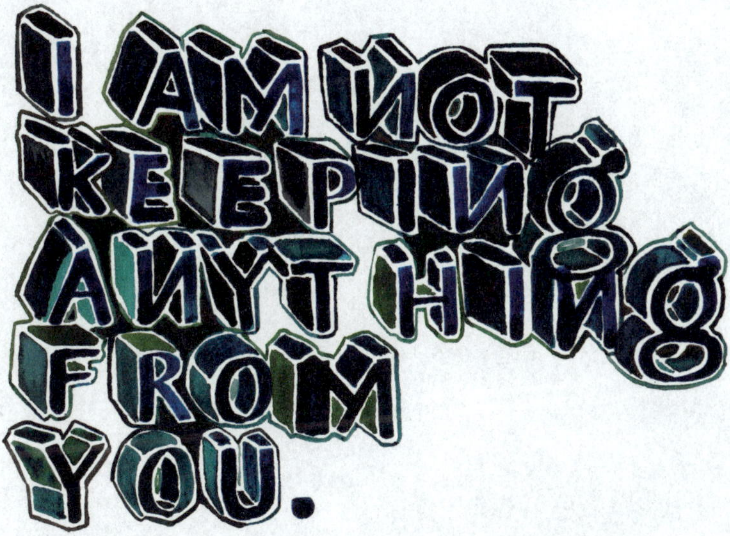
I AM NOT
KEEPING
ANYTHING
FROM
YOU.

If you want to know true gold, test it in the fire. 269

The entire country knows.

wash the inkstone

at the side

of the pond

and

jade lotuses

are

born.

a thousand
errors,
T~~a~~e

a thousand
errors,
ten thousa
nd
mistakes.

It is useless to add extra metal to the head of a needle.

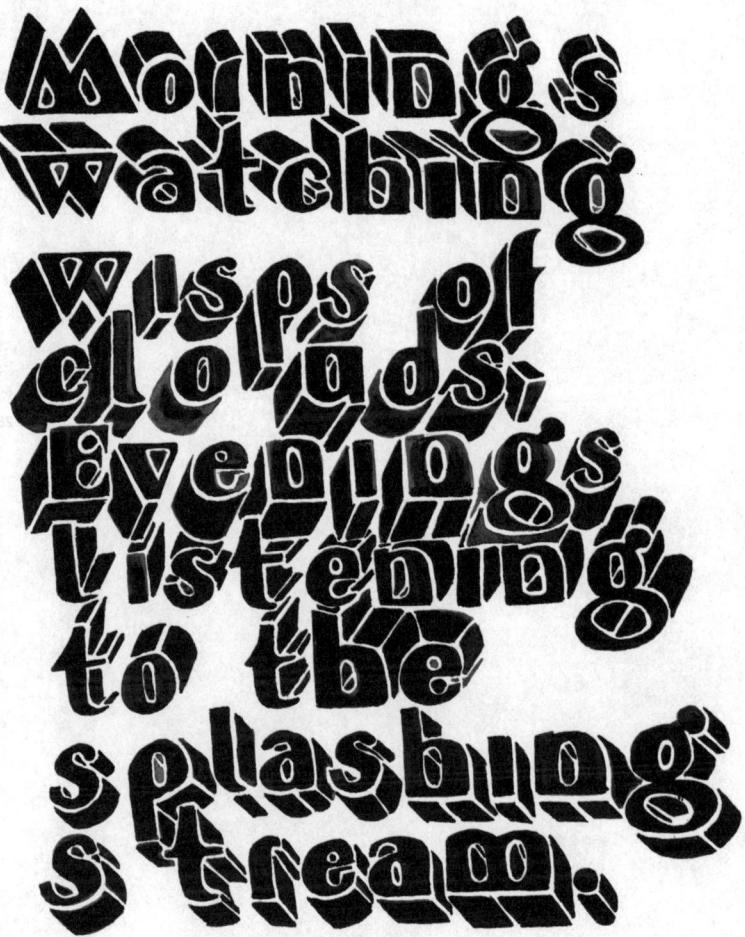

Mornings
watching
wisps of
clouds,
Evenings
listening
to the
splashing
stream.

280

The great earth is so vast,
it saddens people terribly.

The whole body is sickness,
the whole body is medicine.

The fool piles up snow to make a silver mountain. 285

Morning comes, everywhere is the same rain 287
on a thousand houses.

Heaven and hell, the same realm. 289

The sun rises in the east
and at night sets in the west.

292

Gold refined one hundred times does not discolor. 293

To gain an advantage is to be trapped by advantage.

WHAT A PITY,
ALL THAT WORK
FOR NOTHING.

Coming and going, coming and going,
what do you think you are doing?

When you laugh, you cry.

walking,
standing,
sitting,
lying.

It was not courage that kept me behind.
My horses were slow.

Above the saddle no person,
below the saddle no horse.

WATER
AND
MILK
MIX
WITH
EACH
OTHER.

CARVE WORDS
OUT OF MEANING
CARVE ACTIONS
OUT OF WORDS.

SEIZING CLOUDS, GRABBING MIST.

One thing not experienced is one wisdom not gained.

STICK YOUR HEAD OUTSIDE THE SKY, WHO IS THERE TO FACE YOU?

Better not to deceive people.

320

TWO MIRRORS
REFLECT EACH
OTHER;
IN BETWEEN,
THERE IS NO
IMAGE.

AN IRON BULL HAS NO BONES

THINGS
ARISE
OUT OF
POLITENESS.

things
arise
out of
politeness

Have one morning without worry
and forever after be at ease.

Think no thought and all is flawless.

In what public official is there no private feeling? 333
In what stream are there no fish?

Inside nothing to attain, outside nothing to seek. 335

Don't see the strange as strange,
and its strangeness will just disappear.

The wind blows but cannot enter it,
the water falls but cannot wet it.

**When the cold comes, wear more clothes;
when the heat comes, use a fan.**

342

In my eyes, the sound of spring water;
in my ears, the colors of the hills.

What I heard was fabulous wealth,
what I saw was desperate poverty.

Good and bad are like floating clouds, Nowhere do they arise or dissolve.

Good and bad
are like
floating
clouds,
Nowhere
do they
arise or
dissolve.

350

If you don't get your mind off rank,
you will fall in the poison sea.

You can't turn gold into gold,
you can't wet water with water.

Over abro

s hewea

over a br

jacket

s he wea

ade skirt

s net;

cade

s gauze.

Though gold dust is precious, 357
in the eyes it obscures the vision.

358

THE TONGUE FALLS ONTO THE GROUND.

360

I MET AN UNEXPECTED DISASTER.

I met an unexpected disaster.

To maintain focus moment to mome ent is very difficult.

365

TO MAINTA
IN
FOCUS
MOMENT TO
MOMENT IS
VERY
DIFFICULT.

TO maintain focus moment TO moment is very difficult

YOU'RE ONLY HALFWAY.

YOU'RE
only
halfway.

373

YOU'RE ONLY HALFWAY.

Beautiful snow! Flake after flake,
they fall in no other place.

If the heart does not betray others,
the face will not color with shame.

We drunkenly see the ground of actuality as "my world". 381

382

When I look I do not see,
when I listen there is no sound.

Self and other are not two;
in error we create "they" and "I".

When I looked, it seemed to be in front,
and then suddenly it was behind.

One who swims well drowns,
one who rides well falls.

All things in their real aspect—what is there to regret, what is there to hate?

Perfection is like the great emptiness,
nothing lacking and nothing in excess.

With coarse chewing you are quickly satisfied,
with fine chewing you are seldom hungry.

Water freezes and turns to ice,
ice melts and turns to water.

Water doesn't ask for a channel.
A channel doesn't ask for water.

In front, blue waters; behind, green hills. 401

Where water flows, channels form;
when the wind blows, the grasses bend.

From the start it is naturally so,
it does not need any sculpting.

The arrow has already left the bow,
it cannot come back.

In the
fireplace
there is
no host 409
or
guest.

410

Serene and still, like springtime in the flowers. 411

it looks like
a tiger,
but it has
these two
horns;
it looks like
a cow, but
it lacks a
swishy
tail.

it looks like
a tiger,
but it has
these two
horns;
it looks like
a cow, but
it lacks a
swishy
tail.

it looks like
a tiger,
but it has
these two
horns,
it looks like
a cow,
but it lacks
a
swishy
tail.

it looks like
a tiger,
but it has
these two
horns,
it looks like
a cow but
it lacks a
swishy
tail.

iT looks like
a Tiger, buT
iT has These
~~The~~ TWO
horns,
iT looks like
a cow, buT
iT lacks a
swishy
tail.

IT LOOKS LIKE
A TIGER,
BUT IT HAS
THESE TWO
HORNS;
IT LOOKS LIKE
A COW,
BUT IT LACKS
A SWISHY
TAIL.

it looks like
a tiger, but
it has these
two horns; 425
it looks like
a cow, but
it lacks a
swishy tail.

Even the vast
sky and the
broad earth
must some-
day come to
an end,
But this
bitterness
lingers on an
don and does
not cease.

Even the vast sky and the broad earth must someday come to an end,

But this bitterness lingers on and on, and does not cease.

Even the vast sky and the broad earth must someday come to an end,

But this bitterness lingers on and does not cease.

Do not think at all about good and bad.

PUSH, IT WILL NOT GO; PULL, IT WILL NOT COME.

If you lose right thought even a moment, you violate someone else.

beggar-boy
suddenly rich,
stop telling us
your fantasies!
in whose house
is there not
smoke from the
hearth fire?

Vast rumbling thunder and not a drop of rain.

High mountains and deep streams,
quiet clouds and gentle winds.

442

Though no rain falls, blossoms still fall;
though no breeze stirs, willow down floats by.

The bowl fell to the ground and broke into pieces,
seven or eight.

446

Years of built-up burden dropped in a single moment.

A flock of pretty girls, with "moth eyebrows" 449
in broad clear faces,
each carries a flower spray and is clad
in embossed brocade.

Blah, blah, blah, blah, yes and no.

One night the flowers fell in the rain,
and throughout the city the waters flowed fragrant.

Where the sun and shade do not reach,
there is marvelous scenery indeed.

The water a cow drinks turns to milk, 457
the water a snake drinks turns to poison.

Though deathly ill,
I sat hold upright
in shock.
A dark wind
was
driving in rain
through the
cold window.

Though deathly
ill, I sat bold
upright in
shock.
A dark wind
was driving in
rain through
the cold
window.

Though the nation is torn apart, 463
the mountains and rivers remain;
the city in spring is deep in grass and trees.

THE PARROT
CALLS FOR
GREEN TEA,
BUT OFFER TEA
AND IT WON'T
UNDERSTAND.

~~Clear skies~~

clear skies,
a lone goose
in the
distance;
On the broad
ocean,
a single
slow
sail.

468

CLOUDS IN THE SKY WATER IN THE BOTTLE.

When a person
walks over the
bridge,
The bridge flows,
the water doesn't.

The person
without
hands
gives a
good
punch.

474

The grasses are green, green in color; 475
long or short, the spring wind lets them be.

476

Spring wind
Spring rain, and
again the
flowers have
bloomed;
Spring rain,
spring wind, and
again the
flowers have
fallen.

Spring wind,
Spring rain,
and again the
flowers have
bloomed;
Spring rain,
spring wind,
and again the
flowers have
fallen.

480

Spring wind, spring rain,
and again the flowers
have bloomed;
Spring rain, spring
wind, and again the

flowers have fallen.

The whale drinks the wash water from the bowl,
the rhinoceros adjusts the boat of the oil lamp.

484

In the middle of the rain,
see the bright sun shining;
in the midst of fire,
dip from the clear spring.

Even
a
Ton
of
gold
will
dwindle
away.

487

Moved by the moment, I weep even at flowers; 489
sad at parting,
even birds suddenly disturb my heart.

490

NONCHALANTLY
I DROPPED A
LINE
AND STARTLED
AWAKE THE
DRAGON IN
THE DEEP
POOL.

NONCHALANTY
I DROPPEDA
LINE

AND STARTLED
AWAKE THE
DRAGON IN
THE DEEP
POOL.

Good works do not go further than the gate, 495
but bad deeds go a thousand miles.

South of the river, it's a tangerine; north of the river, it's an orange.

SITTING QUIETLY
DOING NOTHING,
SPRING COMES
GRASS GROWS
BY ITSELF.

USE SHRIMPS AS EYES.

ONE

ONE PRINCIPLE COMPLETE EQUALITY.

To attain release from self is easy, 505
but to speak after liberation is difficult.

The blue mountains are just blue mountains,
the white clouds are just white clouds.

The blue mountains by nature are immoveable,
the white clouds of themselves come and go.

510

My acquaintances fill the world, 511
but how many of them really know my mind?

512

The great seas surge with tidal waves, 513
in a thousand rivers, the waters flow backwards.

With things, neither grasp nor let go;
with places, transcend far and near.

When you stretch out both legs and sleep, 517
there is neither false nor true.

Open your mouth and at once you're wrong; 519
move your tongue and at once you transgress.

To destroy—is within me.
To put together—is also within me.

silence
is
truly
effective.

523

ALL THE TIME
I THOUGHT I WAS
OPPOSING YOU,
BUT REALLY IT
WAS YOU WHO
WERE OPPOSING
ME.

SHE ROLLS
DOWN THE
JADE DOOR
CURTAIN,
BUT IT WILL
NOT GO AWAY;
SHE BRUSHES
OFF HER
SILK-POUNDING
BLOCK,
BUT STILL
IT COMES.

Ten years in the forest dreaming,
then by the lake laughing a new laugh.

If you have long arms,
your shirt sleeves are short;
if you have small feet,
your straw sandals are big.

One gives birth
to two,
two gives birth
to three,
three gives birth
to the
⌜ten thousand
things⌝.

ONE GIVES BIRTH
TO TWO,
TWO GIVES BIRTH
TO THREE,
THREE GIVES BIRTH
TO THE
'TEN THOUSAND
THINGS'.

When it's cold, it kills you with cold;
when it's hot, it kills you with heat.

Order at its limit is chaos.

One drop of water, one pellet of ice.

541

You add more spirit when you have spirit,
but that's style when you have no style.

The kitchen and the temple gate.

My! My! Oh my!
But it's not my job to watch people's hair go white.

The sunflower
faces
the sun.

The little fish swallows the big fish.

552

Without the clearing wind to roll away 553
the drifting clouds, how could we see
this vast sky and mile after mile of heaven?

You forget your feet when your shoes
are comfortable.
You forget your waist when your belt
is comfortable.
You forget right and wrong when your mind
is comfortable.

The drowning person is in the water,
the rescuer is in the water.
Their being in the water
is the same,
but their reason for being in the water
is different.

How far are they apart?

560

One arrow, two hits.

There is not even one thing.

Be clever! Be astute! Be alert! 565

To know and yet to transgress.

Words depleted, reason spent.

This

self-satisfied

fellow.

This self-satisfied fellow.

Watch the wind to handle the sail.

576

It is hard to find traces.

It is hard to find traces.

The head of a chicken and the ~~th~~ tail of a phoenix.

One should know propriety. 583

You have seen right to the core. 585

At this step, at that step.

When you love it, you want it to live;
when you hate it, you want it to die.

Before my very eyes, vivid and sharp. 591

592

Look where you're going! Watch where you step! 593

There's no cool spot in a cauldron of boiling water.

Even a good thing isn't as good as nothing. 597

Don't laugh at me lying drunk on the battlefield. 599
How many have ever come back from war?

Like a person's hand in the middle of the night 601
searching behind for the pillow.

in front,

agate;

behind,

pearls.

603

604

HIDE
WORLD
WITHIN
THE
WORLD.

Gone! Those years have all been used up.

608

Chew emptiness to pieces.

North, south, east, west have no door; 611
the great earth, mountains and rivers
conceal nothing.

612

Seven up and down, eight side to side.

614

Seven up and down,

eight

side to side.

615

Seven up and down, eight side to side.

Receive everything as you would receive a single snow-flake in your hand, without fear.

619

620

What is the color of the wind?
Where does the rain come from?

Just this one thought. 623

Try To explain
even one
Thing
and
already
you've missed
The mark.

It's like cutting a bundle of threads—one cut cuts all.

Thunderous snoring, dust flies from the beams.

Ah yes!
Quite obscure.

631

At times you sit atop the lone mountain peak and
let your hands dangle into the busy intersection;
at times, while in the busy intersection,
you drowse off on the lone mountain peak.

don't fantasize

don't fantasize.

don't
fantasize.

don't
fantasize.

Dont fanta-size.

Go and become the incense burner in the old shrine.

646

Dead tree,
cold ashes.

Don't mistake a green cloud for a colored phoenix, 649
and stop taking willow down for flying snow.

650

Listen to the sound of a single hand (clapping). 651

As for resemblance, it certainly resembles; 653
but as for being it, it certainly is not.

654

Its head is long—three feet; 655
its legs are short—one inch;
it faces me in silence standing on one leg.

656

Our sect has neither word nor transmission; 657
from here, the road to India
is eight thousand miles.

658

Have a shit, take a piss. 659

660

Equality without discrimination
is not the Buddha-dharma—it is bad equality.
Discrimination without equality
is not the Buddha-dharma—it is bad discrimination.

662

Keep a lamp lit in a dark room.

Empty-handed, grasp the spade; 665
while walking on foot, ride the water buffalo;
when a person walks over the bridge,
the bridge flows, the water doesn't.

In the honey There's arsenic.

In the
honey
There's
arsenic.

On the third day, she goes down to the kitchen 671
and washes her hands to make the stew.
She hasn't yet learned her mother-in-law's
taste in food and asks her sister-in-law
to check the flavor.

As ignorant as a rub of lacquer.

673

The walls have ears. 675

Little compassion obstructs great compassion.

677

The pine Tree, a Thousand years of green.

Those sitting see those standing,
those standing see those sitting.

In the abandoned house, not a person to be seen. 683
The reeds are broken
and where have the geese gone?

684

Like drinking water and knowing for yourself 685
hot and cold.

Pretty lady of Chao, stirred by the spring, 687
climbs the painted pavilion.
With just one song,
her voice fills the city with autumn.

688

For example, it is like brocade weaving: 689
Both front and back are flowers.

690

If mother is here, then one child is cold; 691
if mother is gone, won't three children be cold?

My wife rocks her loom clack-clack,
my baby plays with its mouth ga-ga.

694

Last year's poverty wasn't quite poverty,
but this year's poverty is really poverty.

Your own nostrils received at birth from 697
your parents are in someone else's hands.

698

No need to do
it again.

She says to herself, 701
"My beautiful face is hard to match."
Then coming to the clothes rack,
she puts on a robe of sheer silk.

Make do with little.

Not wanting to discolor her face
with rouge and powder,
she lightly brushes her "moth eyebrows"
and goes to an audience with the emperor.

706

Where the fish goes, the water is murky.

Upset lakes, overturn mountains.

Upset
lakes,
overturn
mountains.

If you want to see her endless discontent at spring, 713
it's all there when her needle stops in silence.

714

The sky colt races thousands of miles in a day;
back and forth, far and wide,
it gallops as fast as flying.

Empty mountains, 717
no trace of my coming and going.
Some other day we shall meet—but where?

718

The golden needle has never revealed its point, 719
but it draws the threadless jade thread out long.

720

To take what's coming to you and get out. 721

Words fail.

The lion on one hair
displays itself on one billion hairs.

Get your feet on solid ground. 727

ALREADY
SWALLOWED
IT.

Remote and free, not caught up in things.

731

REMOTE AND FREE, NOT CAUGHT UP IN THINGS.

When alive
your wealth
is the dew
on the grass;
After
death, your
fame is the
flowers by
the
roadside.

736

Reason is at its limits, feeling and intellect 737
forgotten—what can be likened to this?

738

Through the
pure waves
There's no
path.

Trough The
pure waves
There's no path.

743

PAGE		CAPPING PHRASE
11–15	E	Easy to call hard to send away.
	D	Leicht zu rufen, schwer wegzuschicken.
	F	Facile à appeler, difficile à renvoyer.
17	D	„Feuer" zu sagen, verbrennt nicht deinen Mund; „Wasser" zu sagen, ertränkt dich nicht.
	F	Dire « feu » ne brûle pas la bouche ; dire « eau » ne vous noie pas.
19	E	Follow the tides and ride the waves.
	D	Folge den Gezeiten und reite die Wellen.
	F	Suis les marées et monte les vagues.
21	E	Like a shooting spark, like a flash of lightening.
	D	Wie ein schießender Funke, wie ein Lichtblitz.
	F	Comme une étincelle de tir, comme un éclair.
23	D	Eine Begegnung: ein für alle Mal.
	F	Une rencontre : une fois pour toutes.
25	D	Sich verbeugen und zurückziehen.
	F	S'incliner et se retirer.
27, 29	E	The scarecrow keeps standing holding a bow and arrow even after the harvest is over.
	D	Die Vogelscheuche bleibt stehen und hält Pfeil und Bogen, auch nachdem die Ernte vorüber ist.
	F	L'épouvantail reste debout tenant un arc et une flèche même après la récolte.
31	D	Ein Staubkorn im Auge: illusorische Blumen tanzen wild.
	F	Un grain de poussière dans l'œil : des fleurs illusoires dansent follement.
33	E	Buying high, selling low.
	D	Teuer kaufen, günstig verkaufen.
	F	Acheter à haut prix, vendre à bas prix.
35	D	Ein Zoll Schildkrötenhaar wiegt sieben Pfund.
	F	Un pouce de poil de tortue pèse sept livres.
37, 39	E	Seven times take in, eight times let go.
	D	Siebenmal nehmen, achtmal loslassen.
	F	Sept fois prendre, huit fois lâcher.
41	D	Nicht zu wissen ist das Vertrauteste.
	F	Ne pas savoir est ce qu'il y a de plus intime.

PAGE		CAPPING PHRASE
43	D	Reite nicht auf Dingen herum, die abgeschlossen sind.
	F	Ne pas ressasser ce qui est terminé.
45	D	Wer gutes Wissen hat, muss auch gut handeln.
	F	Celle qui sait bien doit agir bien.
47	D	Ein Gespann von Pferden kann ein einmal ausgesprochenes Wort nicht einfangen.
	F	Une harde de chevaux ne peut rattraper un mot déjà prononcé.
49	D	Ein Mond zeigt sich in jedem Teich; in jedem Teich der eine Mond.
	F	Une lune se montre dans chaque bassin ; dans chaque bassin, la même lune.
51	D	Sprechen, ohne zu sprechen, wissen, ohne zu wissen.
	F	Parler sans parler, savoir sans savoir.
53	D	Nicht dies, nicht dies, nicht dies.
	F	Pas ceci, pas cela, pas ceci.
55	D	Eine Lampe, zehntausend Lampen, Lampe um Lampe ohne Ende.
	F	Une lampe, dix mille lampes, lampe après lampe sans fin.
57	D	Wasser wäscht kein Wasser; Gold verwandelt sich nicht in Gold.
	F	L'eau ne lave pas l'eau ; l'or ne se transforme pas en or.
59	E	This error, that error.
	D	Dieser Fehler, jener Fehler.
	F	Cette erreur ici, cette erreur là.
61	D	Worte erschöpft; Vernunft verbraucht.
	F	Mots épuisés ; raison épuisée.
63, 65	E	One thousand acts, ten thousand impulses moving all at once.
	D	Tausend Handlungen, zehntausend Impulse, die sich alle auf einmal in Bewegung setzen.
	F	Mille actions, dix mille impulsions se déplaçant toutes à la fois.
67–71	E	Don't blame the past.
	D	Gib nicht der Vergangenheit Schuld.
	F	Ne blâme pas le passé.

PAGE		CAPPING PHRASE
73	D	Noch nicht! Überhaupt nicht. Niemals.
	F	Pas encore ! Pas du tout. Jamais.
75	D	Ich brauche nicht einmal eine Sache, geschweige denn zwei oder drei.
	F	Je n'ai pas besoin même d'une chose, encore moins de deux ou trois.
77	D	Der Donner grollt einmal: ein klarer Wind erhebt sich.
	F	Le tonnerre gronde une fois : un vent clair se lève.
79	D	Bewahre die ganze Welt in einem Hirsekorn auf! Koche Berge und Flüsse in einem Zwei-Liter-Topf.
	F	Garde le monde entier dans un grain de millet ! Fais bouillir montagnes et rivières dans un pot de deux litres.
81	D	Blaue Berge nach dem Regenfall – viel blauer.
	F	Des montagnes bleues après la pluie – bien plus bleues.
83	D	Wühle nicht auf, was bereits erledigt ist.
	F	Ne pas ressasser ce qui est déjà fait.
85	D	Ein einmal ausgesprochenes Wort kann von schnellen Pferden nicht eingefangen werden.
	F	Un mot une fois prononcé ne peut être rattrapé même par des chevaux rapides.
87	D	Erscheinen wie Geister und verschwinden wie Gespenster.
	F	Apparaître comme des esprits et disparaître comme des fantômes.
89	E	Whatever you touch is refreshing.
	D	Was auch immer du berührst, ist erfrischend.
	F	Tout ce que tu touches est rafraîchissant.
91	D	Bar aller persönlichen Besitztümer.
	F	Dépouillée de toutes les possessions personnelles.
93	E	Forget before, lose track after.
	D	Vergiss vorher, verliere den Überblick danach.
	F	Oublie avant, perds la trace après.
95	E	Add where there's lots, reduce where there's little.
	D	Füge dort hinzu, wo viel ist, reduziere dort, wo wenig ist.
	F	Ajoute où il y a beaucoup, réduis où il y a peu.

PAGE		CAPPING PHRASE
97	E	Lose both host and guest.
	D	Verliere sowohl Gastgeberin als auch Gästin.
	F	Perds à la fois l'hôtesse et la convive.
99–103	E	I have no comment.
	D	Ich habe keinen Kommentar.
	F	Je n'ai pas de commentaire.
105	D	Seit tausend Zeitaltern keine Antwort.
	F	Depuis mille âges, pas de réponse.
107	D	Erklärte es weg.
	F	Expliquée et terminée.
109	D	Makellos, durchsichtig.
	F	Immaculée, transparente.
111	D	Herz offenbart, nackt und rot.
	F	Cœur exposé, nu et rouge.
113	D	Es ist verboten, alles zu erzählen.
	F	Il est interdit de tout dire.
115	D	Unverkaufte Waren, tausend Jahre alt.
	F	Marchandises invendues vieilles de mille ans.
117	D	Es gibt Erleuchtung, es gibt Handeln.
	F	Il y a de l'illumination, il y a de l'action.
119	D	Viel zu sorgfältig.
	F	Beaucoup trop méticuleuse.
121	D	Von Angesicht zu Angesicht, tausend Meilen entfernt.
	F	Face à face, à mille lieues de distance.
123	D	Die große Erde hat kein Draußen.
	F	La grande terre n'a pas de dehors.
125	D	Wie es jetzt ist.
	F	Tel que c'est maintenant.
127	D	Wenn du von Angesicht zu Angesicht bist, ist es schwer, dich zu verbergen.
	F	Quand vous êtes face à face, il t'est difficile de te cacher.
129	D	Ein Wassertropfen wird zu einer Eisperle.
	F	Une goutte d'eau devient une perle de glace.

PAGE		CAPPING PHRASE
131	D	Im Spiegel des Himmels gibt es kein eigenes Selbst.
	F	Dans le miroir du ciel, il n'y a pas de soi privé.
133	D	Geht in den Schlamm, geht ins Wasser.
	F	Va dans la boue, va dans l'eau.
135	D	Wenn man alt wird, wird das Herz einsam.
	F	Avec l'âge, le cœur devient solitaire.
137	D	Pass auf dem Weg auf Dich auf.
	F	Prends soin de toi en chemin.
139–145	E	Mind and things are both forgotten.
	D	Verstand und Dinge sind beide vergessen.
	F	L'esprit et les choses sont toutes deux oubliées.
147	D	Inwiefern ist es weit weg?
	F	Dans quel sens est-ce loin ?
149	E	Mild as a clean breeze.
	D	Mild wie eine frische Brise.
	F	Douce comme une brise propre.
151	E	What is this before your very eyes?
	D	Was ist das vor deinen Augen?
	F	Qu'est-ce que c'est devant tes propres yeux ?
153	D	Warum in solch einer schrecklichen Eile?
	F	Pourquoi en hâte si fébrile ?
155	D	Natürlich und ohne Anstrengung.
	F	Naturellement et sans effort.
157	D	Ergreife und halte fest, lasse los und lasse gehen.
	F	Saisis et tiens fermement, relâche et laisse passer.
159	D	Feuer ist heiß, Wasser ist kalt.
	F	Le feu est chaud, l'eau est froide.
161	D	Schlage die Signaltrommel, hol alle zur Hilfe.
	F	Bats le tambour signal, fais aider tout le monde.
163	D	Es gibt keine Erklärung.
	F	Il n'y a aucune explication.
165	D	Wahre Person ohne Rang.
	F	Vraie personne sans rang.

PAGE		CAPPING PHRASE
167	D	Das ist großartig! Das ist schrecklich!
	F	C'est génial ! C'est affreux !
169	E	The post, the lantern.
	D	Der Pfosten, die Laterne.
	F	Le poteau, la lanterne.
171	E	Blue, yellow, red, white, black.
	D	Blau, gelb, rot, weiß, schwarz.
	F	Bleu, jaune, rouge, blanc, noir.
173	E	Totally in action, nothing hidden.
	D	Völlig im Handeln, nichts verborgen.
	F	Totalement en action, rien de caché.
175	D	Welcher Ort kann nicht als Ehrenplatz bezeichnet werden?
	F	Quel endroit ne peut pas être appelé un lieu d'honneur ?
177	D	Ungeboren, unsterblich.
	F	Pas encore né, éternel.
179	D	Schließe deinen Mund und sage ein Wort.
	F	Ferme la bouche et dis un mot.
181	E	Get the question clear and you are already close to the answer.
	D	Stell die Frage klar und schon bist Du nah bei der Antwort.
	F	Comprenez bien la question et vous êtes déjà proche de la réponse.
183	E	A worm cut into two—which half is the true worm?
	D	Ein Wurm in zwei Hälften geschnitten – welche Hälfte ist der wahre Wurm?
	F	Un ver coupé en deux – quelle moitié est le vrai ver ?
185	E	It is inconvenient for me.
	D	Es ist unpassend für mich.
	F	C'est incommode pour moi.
187	D	Zu wissen und dennoch nachzufragen, ist Höflichkeit.
	F	Savoir et pourtant demander est une politesse.
189–193	E	Fire does not dry, water does not wet.
	D	Feuer trocknet nicht, Wasser macht nicht nass.
	F	Le feu ne sèche pas, l'eau ne mouille pas.

PAGE		CAPPING PHRASE
195–199	E	Who would keep you in the dark?
	D	Wer würde dich im Dunkeln lassen?
	F	Qui te maintiendrait dans l'obscurité ?
201	D	Ein Mensch in Trauer weiß, dass die Nacht lang ist.
	F	Une personne triste sait que la nuit est longue.
203	D	Kurz bevor es regnet, scheinen die Berge näher.
	F	Juste avant la pluie, les montagnes semblent plus proches.
205	D	Steinfiguren flüstern sich gegenseitig zu.
	F	Des statues de pierre se chuchotent l'une à l'autre.
207	D	Die wilden Gräser wurden nie geschnitten.
	F	Les herbes sauvages n'ont jamais été coupées.
209	D	Ein Wort des Geständnisses.
	F	Un mot de confession.
211	D	Grundsätzlich gibt es nicht eine einzige Sache.
	F	Fondamentalement, il n'y a pas une seule chose.
213	D	Wenn du das auf Wasser schlägst, verletzt du die Köpfe der Fische.
	F	Si tu tapes l'eau, tu blesses les têtes des poissons.
215	D	Oben, unten und in alle vier Himmelsrichtungen, keine Konkurrentinnen.
	F	En haut, en bas, et dans les quatre directions, pas de rivales.
217	D	Fallende Blumen, fließende Gewässer, unendlich, weitläufig.
	F	Fleurs qui tombent, eaux qui coulent, sans limite, vastes.
219	D	Sehen, ohne zu sehen, hören, ohne zu hören.
	F	Voir sans voir, entendre sans entendre.
221	D	Heute gibt es, morgen gibt es nicht.
	F	Aujourd'hui il y a, demain il n'y en a pas.
223	D	Eine lange Sache ist lang, eine kurze Sache ist kurz.
	F	Une chose longue est longue, une chose courte est courte.
225	D	Die Blume im Garten, ist sie lebendig oder tot?
	F	La fleur dans le jardin, est-elle vivante ou morte ?

PAGE		CAPPING PHRASE
227	D	Berge sind Berge, Flüsse sind Flüsse.
	F	Les montagnes sont des montagnes, les rivières sont des rivières.
229	D	Denke weder gut noch böse.
	F	Ne pense ni bien, ni mal.
231	D	Kiefernnadeln sind nicht gerade, Dornen sind nicht gebogen.
	F	Les aiguilles de pin ne sont pas droites, les épines ne sont pas courbées.
233	E	One, or a half, or ten million.
	D	Eins oder eine Hälfte oder zehn Millionen.
	F	Un, ou une moitié, ou dix millions.
235, 237	E	One who takes careful aim does not hit the target.
	D	Wer sorgfältig zielt, trifft nicht das Ziel.
	F	Celle qui vise avec soin ne touche pas la cible.
239	D	Für böse Worte, die eine Person verletzen, vergeht der Groll nie.
	F	Pour des mots méchants qui blessent une personne, le ressentiment ne s'estompe jamais.
241–247	E	The tongue has no bones.
	D	Die Zunge hat keine Knochen.
	F	La langue n'a pas d'os.
249	D	Ein Regen benetzt alles, bedeckt die ganze Welt.
	F	Une pluie mouille tout, recouvrant le monde entier.
251	D	Wind und Tau und der frische Duft von Chrysanthemen.
	F	Vent et rosée et le parfum frais des chrysanthèmes.
253	D	Oben in den Bäumen öffnet der Karpfen weit seinen Mund und lacht.
	F	Là-haut dans les arbres, la carpe ouvre grand la bouche et rit.
255	D	Grüne Berge nach dem Regen, das Grün ist noch grüner.
	F	Les montagnes vertes après la pluie, le vert est encore plus vert.
257	D	Wie kann ein Sperling das Streben eines wilden Schwans kennen?
	F	Comment un moineau peut-il connaître l'aspiration d'un cygne sauvage ?

PAGE		CAPPING PHRASE
259	D	Gestern hat es geregnet, heute ist es klar.
	F	Hier il a plu, aujourd'hui c'est clair.
261	D	Alle deine Knochen und Gelenke sind aus Gold gemacht.
	F	Tous tes os et articulations sont faites d'or.
263	D	An der belebten Kreuzung, eine abgenutzte Sandale.
	F	À l'intersection animée, une sandale usée.
265, 267	E	I am not keeping anything from you.
	D	Ich halte nichts vor dir zurück.
	F	Je ne te cache rien.
269	D	Wenn du echtes Gold kennen willst, prüfe es im Feuer.
	F	Si tu veux connaître l'or vrai, teste-le dans le feu.
271	E	The entire country knows.
	D	Das ganze Land weiß es.
	F	Tout le pays sait.
273	E	Wash the inkstone at the side of the pond and jade lotuses are born.
	D	Wasche den Tintenstein am Rande des Teiches und Jade-Lotusblumen entstehen.
	F	Lave la pierre à encre au bord de l'étang et des lotus de jade naissent.
275	E	A thousand errors, ten thousand mistakes.
	D	Tausend Irrtümer, zehntausend Fehler.
	F	Mille erreurs, dix mille fautes.
277	D	Es ist nutzlos, zusätzliches Metall dem Kopf einer Nadel hinzuzufügen.
	F	Il est inutile d'ajouter du métal supplémentaire à la tête d'une aiguille.
279	E	Mornings watching wisps of clouds, Evenings listening to the splashing stream.
	D	Morgens Wolkenschwaden beobachten, abends dem plätschernden Bach lauschen.
	F	Des matins à regarder des lambeaux de nuages, des soirées à écouter le ruissellement du ruisseau.
281	D	Die große Erde ist so weitläufig, dass es die Menschen schrecklich betrübt.
	F	La grande terre est si vaste qu'elle attriste terriblement les gens.

283 D Der gesamte Körper ist Krankheit, der gesamte Körper ist Medizin.
F Le corps entier est maladie, le corps entier est remède.

285 D Der Närrin häuft Schnee an, um einen Silberberg zu bauen.
F Le fou amasse de la neige pour construire une montagne d'argent.

287 D Der Morgen kommt, überall ist der gleiche Regen auf tausend Häusern.
F Le matin arrive, partout c'est la même pluie sur mille maisons.

289 D Himmel und Hölle, das gleiche Gebiet.
F Le ciel et l'enfer, le même royaume.

291 D Die Sonne geht im Osten auf und geht nachts im Westen unter.
F Le soleil se lève à l'est et se couche à l'ouest la nuit.

293 D Hundertmal veredeltes Gold verfärbt sich nicht.
F L'or raffiné cent fois ne se décolore pas.

295 D Einen Vorteil zu erlangen, bedeutet, im Vorteil gefangen zu sein.
F Obtenir un avantage, c'est être piégé par l'avantage.

297 E What a pity, all that work for nothing!
D Was für ein Jammer, all diese Arbeit umsonst!
F Quel dommage, tout ce travail pour rien !

299 D Kommen und gehen, kommen und gehen, was glaubst du, was du tust?
F Aller et venir, aller et venir, que pensez-vous être en train de faire ?

301 D Wenn du lachst, weinst du.
F Quand tu ris, tu pleures.

303 E Walking, standing, sitting, lying.
D Gehen, stehen, sitzen, liegen.
F Marcher, rester debout, s'asseoir, être couché.

305 D Es war nicht der Mut, der mich zurückgehalten hat. Meine Pferde waren langsam.
F Ce n'était pas le courage qui m'a retenu. Mes chevaux étaient lents.

PAGE		CAPPING PHRASE
307	D	Über dem Sattel keine Person, unter dem Sattel kein Pferd.
	F	Au-dessus de la selle, aucune personne ; en dessous de la selle, aucun cheval.
309	E	Water and milk mix with each other.
	D	Wasser und Milch vermischen sich miteinander.
	F	L'eau et le lait se mélangent.
311	E	Carve words out of meaning, carve actions out of words.
	D	Schnitze Worte aus Bedeutung, schnitze Handlungen aus Worten.
	F	Sculpte des mots à partir de sens, sculpte des actions à partir de mots.
313	E	Seizing clouds, grabbing mist.
	D	Wolken fassen, Nebel greifen.
	F	Attraper les nuages, saisir la brume.
315	D	Eine Sache, die nicht erlebt wurde, ist eine Weisheit, die nicht erlangt wurde.
	F	Une chose non vécue est une sagesse non acquise.
317	E	Stick your head outside the sky, who is there to face you?
	D	Stecke deinen Kopf aus dem Himmel heraus, wer ist da, um dir zu begegnen?
	F	Sors ta tête du ciel, qui est là pour te faire face ?
319	E	Better not to deceive people.
	D	Es ist besser, Menschen nicht zu täuschen.
	F	Mieux vaut ne pas tromper les gens.
321	E	Two mirrors reflect each other; in between there is no image.
	D	Zwei Spiegel reflektieren sich; dazwischen gibt es kein Bild.
	F	Deux miroirs se reflètent l'un l'autre ; entre eux, il n'y a pas d'image.
323	E	An iron bull has no bones.
	D	Ein eiserner Bulle hat keine Knochen.
	F	Un taureau en fer n'a pas d'os.
325, 327	E	Things arise out of politeness.
	D	Dinge entstehen aus Höflichkeit.
	F	Les choses surgissent par politesse.

329 D Hab einen Morgen ohne Sorgen und sei für immer danach entspannt.
F Aie un matin sans souci et sois pour toujours à l'aise par la suite.

331 D Denke keinen Gedanken, und alles ist makellos.
F Ne pensez aucune pensée et tout est impeccable.

333 D Welche Vertreterin der Öffentlichkeit hat kein privates Gefühl? In welchem Fluss gibt es keine Fische?
F Dans quel fonctionnaire public n'y a-t-il pas de sentiment privé ? Dans quel ruisseau n'y a-t-il pas de poissons ?

335 D Innen nichts zu erreichen, außen nichts zu suchen.
F À l'intérieur rien à atteindre, à l'extérieur rien à chercher.

337 D Sieh das Fremde nicht als fremd an, und seine Fremdheit wird einfach verschwinden.
F Ne voyez pas l'étrange comme étrange, et son étrangeté disparaîtra.

339 D Der Wind weht, aber er kann nicht hinein, das Wasser fließt, aber es kann es nicht durchnässen.
F Le vent souffle mais ne peut y entrer, l'eau coule mais ne peut l'humidifier.

341 D Wenn die Kälte kommt, zieh mehr Kleidung an; wenn die Hitze kommt, benutze einen Fächer.
F Quand le froid arrive, porte plus de vêtements ; quand la chaleur arrive, utilise un éventail.

343 D In meinen Augen der Klang von Quellwasser; in meinen Ohren die Farben der Hügel.
F À mes yeux, le son de l'eau de source ; à mes oreilles, les couleurs des collines.

345 D Was ich hörte, war fabelhafter Reichtum, was ich sah, war verzweifelte Armut.
F Ce que j'ai entendu était une richesse fabuleuse, ce que j'ai vu était une pauvreté désespérée.

347, 349 E Good and bad are like floating clouds; Nowhere do they arise or dissolve.
D Gut und Schlecht sind wie treibende Wolken; nirgendwo entstehen sie oder lösen sie sich auf.
F Le bien et le mal sont comme des nuages flottants ; nulle part ils ne surgissent ni ne se dissolvent.

PAGE		CAPPING PHRASE
351	D	Wenn du deinen Geist nicht aus dem Weg räumst, fällst du ins giftige Meer.
	F	Si tu ne dégages pas ton esprit de tout rang, tu tomberas dans la mer empoisonnée.
353	D	Du kannst Gold nicht in Gold umwandeln, du kannst Wasser nicht mit Wasser befeuchten.
	F	On ne peut pas transformer l'or en or, on ne peut pas mouiller l'eau avec de l'eau.
354–355	E	Over a brocade skirt she wears net; over a brocade jacket she wears gauze.
	D	Über einem Brokatrock trägt sie Netz; über einer Brokatjacke trägt sie Gaze.
	F	Sur une jupe de brocart, elle porte du filet ; sur une veste de brocart, elle porte de la gaze.
357	D	Obwohl Goldstaub kostbar ist, trübt er in den Augen die Sicht.
	F	Bien que la poussière d'or soit précieuse, elle obscurcit la vision.
359	E	The tongue falls onto the ground.
	D	Die Zunge fällt auf den Boden.
	F	La langue tombe par terre.
361, 363	E	I met an unexpected disaster.
	D	Ich traf auf eine unerwartete Katastrophe.
	F	J'ai rencontré un désastre inattendu.
365–369	E	To maintain focus moment to moment is very difficult.
	D	In jedem Moment den Fokus aufrechtzuerhalten, ist sehr schwierig.
	F	Maintenir la concentration d'un moment à l'autre est très difficile.
371–375	E	You're only halfway
	D	Das ist erst die Hälfte.
	F	Tu n'es qu'à mi-chemin.
377	D	Schöner Schnee! Flocke für Flocke fällt er an keinem anderen Ort.
	F	Belle neige ! Flocon après flocon, elle tombe à aucun autre endroit.

PAGE		CAPPING PHRASE
379	D	Wenn das Herz andere nicht verrät, wird das Gesicht nicht vor Scham erröten.
	F	Si le cœur ne trahit pas les autres, le visage ne rougira pas de honte.
381	D	Wir sehen betrunken den Boden der Wirklichkeit als „meine Welt".
	F	Ivres, nous voyons le fond de la réalité comme « mon monde ».
383	D	Wenn ich schaue, sehe ich nicht, wenn ich zuhöre, gibt es keinen Ton.
	F	Quand je regarde, je ne vois pas, quand j'écoute il n'y a pas de son.
385	D	Das Selbst und die Anderen sind nicht zwei; irrtümlich schaffen wir „sie" und „ich".
	F	Soi et l'autre ne sont pas deux ; dans l'erreur nous créons « elles » et « moi ».
387	D	Als ich hinschaute, schien es vorne zu sein, und dann war es plötzlich hinten.
	F	Quand j'ai regardé, il semblait être devant, et puis soudain il était derrière.
389	D	Wer gut schwimmen kann, ertrinkt, wer gut reiten kann, fällt.
	F	Celle qui nage bien se noie, celle qui monte bien tombe.
391	D	Alle Dinge unter ihrem realen Aspekt – was gibt es da zu bedauern, was zu hassen?
	F	Toutes choses dans leur aspect réel – quoi regretter, quoi haïr ?
393	D	Vollkommenheit ist wie die große Leere, nichts fehlt und nichts ist im Übermaß.
	F	La perfection est comme la grande vacuité, rien ne manque et rien n'est en excès.
395	D	Mit grobem Kauen bist du schnell zufrieden, mit feinem Kauen bist du selten hungrig.
	F	Avec une mastication grossière, on est rapidement satisfait, avec une mastication fine on a rarement faim.
397	D	Wasser friert ein und wird zu Eis, Eis schmilzt und wird zu Wasser.
	F	L'eau gèle et devient de la glace, la glace fond et devient de l'eau.

PAGE		CAPPING PHRASE
399	D	Wasser fragt nicht nach einem Kanal. Ein Kanal fragt nicht nach Wasser.
	F	L'eau ne demande pas un canal. Un canal ne demande pas de l'eau.
401	D	Vorne blaue Gewässer; hinten grüne Hügel.
	F	Devant, des eaux bleues ; derrière, des collines vertes.
403	D	Wo Wasser fließt, bilden sich Kanäle; wenn der Wind bläst, biegen sich die Gräser.
	F	Là où l'eau coule se forment des canaux ; quand le vent souffle, l'herbe se plie.
405	D	Es ist von Anfang an auf natürliche Weise so, es muss nicht gestaltet werden.
	F	Dès le départ c'est naturellement ainsi, cela n'a pas besoin d'élaboration.
407	D	Der Pfeil hat bereits den Bogen verlassen, er kann nicht zurückkommen.
	F	La flèche est déjà partie de l'arc, elle ne peut pas retourner.
409	E	In the fireplace there is no host or guest.
	D	Im Kamin gibt es keine Gastgeberin oder Gästin.
	F	Dans la cheminée, il n'y a ni hôtesse ni invitée.
411	D	Gelassen und ruhig, wie Frühling in den Blumen.
	F	Serein et immobile, comme le printemps dans les fleurs.
413–425	E	It looks like a tiger but it has these two horns, it looks like a cow but it lacks a swishy tail.
	D	Es sieht wie ein Tiger aus, aber es hat diese beiden Hörner, es sieht wie eine Kuh aus, aber es fehlt ein schweifartiger Schwanz.
	F	Ça ressemble à un tigre mais il a ces deux cornes, ça ressemble à une vache mais ça manque d'une queue qui remue.
427, 429	E	Even the vast sky and the broad earth must someday come to an end, but this bitterness lingers on and on and does not cease.
	D	Selbst der weite Himmel und die breite Erde müssen irgendwann enden, aber diese Bitterkeit hält an und an und hört nicht auf.
	F	Même le vaste ciel et la large terre doivent un jour prendre fin, mais cette amertume persiste et ne cesse pas.

431 D Denke überhaupt nicht über Gut und Böse nach.
F Ne pensez pas du tout au bien et au mal.

433 E Push, it will not go. Pull, it will not come.
D Stoß, es wird nicht weggehen. Zieh, und es wird nicht mitkommen.
F Pousse, ça n'ira pas. Tire, ça ne viendra pas.

435 D Wenn du auch nur einen Moment das richtige Denken verlierst, verletzt du jemand anderen.
F Si tu perds une seule fois la bonne pensée, tu violes quelqu'un d'autre.

437 E Beggar-boy suddenly rich, stop telling us your fantasies! In whose house is there not smoke from the hearth fire?
D Bettelknabe plötzlich reich, hör auf, uns deine Fantasien zu erzählen! In wessen Haus gibt es keinen Rauch vom Herdfeuer?
F Le mendiant soudainement riche, arrête de nous raconter tes fantasmes ! Dans quelle maison n'y a-t-il pas de fumée du feu de la cheminée ?

439 E Vast rumbling thunder and not a drop of rain.
D Gewaltig donnerndes Gewitter und kein Tropfen Regen.
F Tonnerre grondant énorme et pas une goutte de pluie.

441 D Hohe Berge und tiefe Ströme, ruhige Wolken und sanfte Winde.
F Hautes montagnes et rivières profondes, nuages tranquilles et vents doux.

443 D Obwohl kein Regen fällt, fallen dennoch Blüten; obwohl keine Brise weht, treibt Weidenflaum vorbei.
F Même s'il ne pleut pas, les fleurs tombent toujours ; même si la brise ne souffle pas, des flocons de saule flottent.

445 D Die Schüssel fiel auf den Boden und brach in Stücke, sieben oder acht.
F Le bol est tombé par terre et s'est brisé en morceaux, sept ou huit.

447 D Jahre aufgebauter Last fielen in einem einzigen Moment ab.
F Des années de fardeau accumulé tombaient en un seul moment.

449 D Eine Schar hübscher Mädchen, mit „Schmetterlingsbrauen" in breiten klaren Gesichtern, jede trägt einen Blumenzweig und ist in geprägtem Brokat gekleidet.
F Un groupe de jolies filles, avec des «sourcils de papillon» dans de larges visages clairs, chacune porte une branche de fleurs et est vêtue de brocart en relief.

451 D Blah, blah, blah, blah, ja und nein.
F Bla bla bla bla, oui et non.

453 D Eines nachts fielen die Blumen im Regen, und in der ganzen Stadt flossen duftende Gewässer.
F Une nuit, les fleurs sont tombées sous la pluie, et dans toute la ville, les eaux coulaient parfumées.

455 D Dort, wo Sonne und Schatten nicht hinkommen, gibt es tatsächlich wunderbare Landschaften.
F Là où le soleil et l'ombre ne parviennent pas, il y a vraiment un paysage merveilleux.

457 D Das Wasser, das eine Kuh trinkt, wird zu Milch; das Wasser, das eine Schlange trinkt, wird zu Gift.
F L'eau qu'une vache boit se transforme en lait; l'eau qu'un serpent boit se transforme en poison.

459, 461 E Though deathly ill, I sat bold upright in shock. A dark wind was driving in rain through the cold window.
D Obwohl tödlich krank, saß ich schockiert aufrecht. Ein dunkler Wind trieb Regen durch das kalte Fenster.
F Bien que gravement malade, j'étais assise bien droit, choquée. Un vent sombre chassait la pluie à travers la fenêtre froide.

463 D Obwohl das Land zerrissen ist, bleiben die Berge und Flüsse bestehen; die Stadt im Frühling ist voller in Gras und Bäumen.
F Bien que la nation soit déchirée, les montagnes et les rivières restent ; la ville au printemps est profonde en herbes et arbres.

465 E The parrot calls for green tea, but offer tea and it won't understand.
D Der Papagei ruft nach grünem Tee, aber wenn du ihm Tee anbietest wird er es nicht verstehen.
F Le perroquet demande du thé vert, mais offre-lui du thé et il ne comprendra pas.

467 E Clear skies, a lone goose in the distance, on the broad ocean, a single slow sail.

D Klarer Himmel, eine einsame Gans in der Ferne, auf dem weiten Ozean, ein einziges ruhiges Segel.

F Un ciel clair, une oie solitaire au loin, sur le vaste océan, une seule voile lente.

469 E Clouds in the sky, water in the bottle.

D Wolken am Himmel, Wasser in der Flasche.

F Des nuages dans le ciel, de l'eau dans la bouteille.

471 E When a person walks over the bridge, the bridge flows, the water doesn't.

D Wenn eine Person über die Brücke geht, fließt die Brücke, das Wasser nicht.

F Quand une personne marche sur le pont, le pont coule, l'eau ne le fait pas.

473 E The person without hands gives a good punch. 762

D Die Person ohne Hände gibt einen guten Faustschlag.

F La personne sans mains donne un bon coup de poing.

475 D Die Gräser sind grün, grün in der Farbe; lang oder kurz, der Frühlingswind lässt sie sein.

F Les herbes sont vertes, vertes en couleur ; longues ou courtes, le vent du printemps les laisse être.

477–481 E Spring wind, spring rain, and again the flowers have bloomed; Spring rain, spring wind, and again the flowers have fallen.

D Frühlingswind, Frühlingsregen, und wieder sind die Blumen erblüht; Frühlingsregen, Frühlingswind, und wieder sind die Blumen abgefallen.

F Vent de printemps, pluie de printemps, et encore une fois les fleurs ont fleuri ; pluie de printemps, vent de printemps, et encore une fois les fleurs sont tombées.

483 D Der Wal trinkt das Waschwasser aus der Schüssel, das Nashorn richtet das Schiffchen der Öllampe.

F La baleine boit l'eau de lavage du bol, le rhinocéros ajuste le bateau de la lampe à huile.

485 D Mitten im Regen sieh die strahlende Sonne scheinen; mitten im Feuer schöpfe aus der klaren Quelle.

F Au milieu de la pluie, vois le soleil brillant ; au milieu du feu, puise dans la source claire.

487 E Even a ton of gold will dwindle away.
D Selbst eine Tonne Gold wird schwinden.
F Même une tonne d'or va disparaître.

489 D Ergriffen vom Augenblick, weine ich sogar um die Blumen; traurig über den Abschied, verstören sogar Vögel plötzlich mein Herz.
F Ému par le moment, je pleure même devant les fleurs ; triste à la séparation, même les oiseaux perturbent soudainement mon cœur.

491, 493 E Nonchalantly I dropped a line and startled awake the dragon in the deep pool.
D Unbekümmert ließ ich eine Leine fallen und schreckte den Drachen im tiefen Teich auf.
F Nonchalamment, j'ai lâché une ligne et j' ai réveillé le dragon dans le bassin profond.

495 D Gute Taten gehen nicht weiter als das Tor, aber böse Taten gehen tausend Meilen.
F Les bonnes actions ne vont pas plus loin que la porte, mais les mauvaises actions parcourent mille lieues.

497 D Südlich des Flusses ist es eine Mandarine; nördlich des Flusses ist es eine Orange.
F Au sud de la rivière, c'est une mandarine ; au nord de la rivière, c'est une orange.

499 E Sitting quietly doing nothing, spring comes,
Grass grows by itself.
D Still sitzen und nichts tun, der Frühling kommt,
das Gras wächst von selbst.
F Assise tranquillement sans rien faire, le printemps arrive, l'herbe pousse d'elle-même.

501 E Use shrimps as eyes.
D Verwende Garnelen als Augen.
F Utilise des crevettes comme des yeux.

503 E One principle, complete equality.
D Ein Prinzip, vollständige Gleichheit.
F Un principe, une égalité complète.

505 D Die Befreiung vom Selbst zu erlangen, ist einfach, aber nach der Befreiung zu sprechen, ist schwierig.
F Atteindre la libération du soi est facile, mais parler après la libération est difficile.

PAGE		CAPPING PHRASE
507	D	Die blauen Berge sind einfach blaue Berge, die weißen Wolken sind einfach weiße Wolken.
	F	Les montagnes bleues ne sont que des montagnes bleues, les nuages blancs ne sont que des nuages blancs.
509	D	Die blauen Berge sind von Natur aus unbeweglich, die weißen Wolken kommen und gehen von selbst.
	F	Les montagnes bleues sont immobiles par nature, les nuages blancs viennent et vont d'eux-mêmes.
511	D	Meine Bekannten füllen die Welt, aber wie viele von ihnen kennen wirklich meinen Geist?
	F	Mes connaissances remplissent le monde, mais combien d'entre elles connaissent vraiment mon esprit ?
513	D	Die großen Meere schwellen mit Flutwellen, in tausend Flüssen fließt das Wasser rückwärts.
	F	Les grandes mers déferlent avec des vagues de marée, dans mille rivières, les eaux coulent en arrière. 764
515	D	Die Dinge nicht festhalten und nicht loslassen; bei den Orten über das Nahe und Ferne hinausgehen.
	F	Avec les choses, ni saisir ni lâcher ; avec les lieux, transcender loin et près.
517	D	Wenn du beide Beine ausstreckst und schläfst, gibt es weder falsch noch richtig.
	F	Quand tu allonges tes deux jambes et dors, il n'y a ni faux ni vrai.
519	D	Öffne deinen Mund und schon liegst du falsch; bewege deine Zunge und schon bist du im Unrecht.
	F	Ouvre la bouche et tout de suite tu as tort ; bouge ta langue et tout de suite tu transgresses.
521	D	Zu zerstören – liegt in mir. Aufbauen – liegt auch in mir.
	F	Détruire – est en moi. Réunir – est aussi en moi.
523	E	Silence is truly effective.
	D	Stille ist wirklich effektiv.
	F	Le silence est vraiment efficace.
525	E	All the time I thought I was opposing you, but really it was you who were opposing me.
	D	Die ganze Zeit dachte ich, ich wäre gegen dich, aber in Wirklichkeit warst du es, die gegen mich war.
	F	Tout le temps, je pensais t'opposer, mais c'était vraiment toi qui m'opposais.

527 E She rolls down the jade door curtain, but it will not go away; she brushes off her silk-pounding block, but still it comes.
D Sie rollt den jadefarbenen Türvorhang herunter, aber es geht nicht weg; sie wischt ihren Seidenklopfer ab, aber immer noch kommt er.
F Elle baisse le rideau en jade, mais il ne partira pas ; elle écarte son bloc de frappe de soie, mais il vient toujours.

529 D Zehn Jahre im Wald träumend, dann am See ein neues Lachen lachen.
F Dix ans dans la forêt à rêver, puis près du lac rire un nouveau rire.

531 D Wenn du lange Arme hast, sind deine Hemdsärmel kurz; wenn du kleine Füße hast, sind deine Strohsandalen groß.
F Si tu as de longs bras, tes manches de chemise sont courtes ; si tu as de petits pieds, tes sandales en paille sont grandes.

533, 535 E One gives birth to two, two gives birth to three, three gives birth to the "ten thousand things".
D Eins gebiert zwei, zwei gebiert drei, drei gebiert die „zehntausend Dinge".
F Un donne naissance à deux, deux donne naissance à trois, trois donne naissance aux « dix mille choses ».

537 D Wenn es kalt ist, tötet es dich mit Kälte; wenn es heiß ist, tötet es dich mit Hitze.
F Quand il fait froid, ça te tue avec le froid ; quand il fait chaud, ça te tue avec la chaleur.

539 D Ordnung an ihrer Spitze ist Chaos.
F L'ordre à son extrême est le chaos.

541 E One drop of water, one pellet of ice.
D Ein Tropfen Wasser, ein Granulat Eis.
F Une goutte d'eau, un granule de glace.

543 D Man fügt mehr Geist hinzu, wenn man Geist hat, aber das ist Stil, wenn man keinen Stil hat.
F Tu ajoutes plus d'esprit quand tu as de l'esprit, mais c'est du style quand tu n'en as pas.

545 E The kitchen and the temple gate.
D Die Küche und das Tempeltor.
F La cuisine et la porte du temple.

547 D Meine Güte! Meine Güte! Oje! Aber es ist nicht meine Aufgabe, zu beobachten, wie das Haar anderer ergraut.
F Mon Dieu ! Oh mon Dieu ! Mais ce n'est pas mon travail de regarder les cheveux des gens blanchir.

549 E The sunflower faces the sun.
D Die Sonnenblume zeigt zur Sonne.
F Le tournesol fait face au soleil.

551 E The little fish swallows the big fish.
D Der kleine Fisch verschlingt den großen Fisch.
F Le petit poisson avale le gros poisson.

553 D Ohne den klärenden Wind, der die treibenden Wolken vertreibt, wie könnten wir diesen weiten Himmel und Meile um Meile vom Himmel sehen?
F Sans le vent dégagé pour chasser les nuages en dérive, comment pourrions-nous voir ce vaste ciel et mile après mile du ciel ?

555 D Du vergisst deine Füße, wenn deine Schuhe bequem sind. Du vergisst deine Gürtellinie, wenn dein Gürtel bequem ist. Du vergisst richtig und falsch, wenn dein Geist bequem ist.
F Tu oublies tes pieds quand tes chaussures sont confortables. Tu oublies ta taille quand ta ceinture est confortable. Tu oublies le bien et le mal quand ton esprit est confortable.

557 D Die ertrinkende Person ist im Wasser, die Retterin ist im Wasser. Ihre Anwesenheit im Wasser ist gleich, aber ihr Grund dafür, im Wasser zu sein, ist unterschiedlich.
F La personne qui se noie est dans l'eau, le sauveteur est dans l'eau. Leur être dans l'eau est le même, mais leur raison d'être dans l'eau est différente.

559 D Wie weit sind sie voneinander entfernt?
F A quelle distance sont-elles l'un de l'autre ?

561 D Ein Pfeil, zwei Treffer.
F Une flèche, deux coups.

563 D Es gibt nicht einmal eine Sache.
F Il n'y a même pas une seule chose.

565 D Sei schlau! Sei scharfsinnig! Sei wachsam!
F Sois intelligente ! Sois astucieuse ! Sois attentive !

PAGE		CAPPING PHRASE
567	D	Zu wissen und dennoch zu überschreiten.
	F	Savoir et pourtant transgresser.
569	D	Worte aufgebraucht, Vernunft erschöpft.
	F	Mots épuisés, raison épuisée.
571, 573	E	This self-satisfied fellow.
	D	Diese selbstzufriedene Kollegin.
	F	Cette personne satisfaite de soi.
575	D	Beobachte den Wind, um das Segel zu steuern.
	F	Observe le vent pour manipuler la voile.
577, 579	E	It is hard to find traces.
	D	Es ist schwer, Spuren zu finden.
	F	Il est difficile de trouver des traces.
581	E	The head of a chicken and the tail of a phoenix.
	D	Der Kopf eines Huhns und der Schwanz eines Phönix.
	F	La tête d'un poulet et la queue d'un phénix.
583	D	Man sollte Anstand kennen.
	F	On devrait connaître la bienséance.
585	D	Du hast bis zum Kern richtig gesehen.
	F	Tu as vu juste au cœur des choses.
587	D	Bei diesem Schritt, bei jenem Schritt.
	F	À cette étape ici, à cette étape là.
589	D	Wenn du sie liebst, willst du, dass sie lebt; wenn du sie hasst, willst du, dass sie stirbt.
	F	Quand tu l'aimes, tu veux qu'elle vive ; quand tu la détestes, tu veux qu'elle meurt.
591	D	Vor meinen Augen, lebendig und scharf.
	F	Sous mes yeux, vif et net.
593	D	Schau, wohin du gehst! Achte darauf, wohin du trittst!
	F	Regarde où tu vas ! Fais attention où tu mets les pieds !
595	D	Es gibt keinen kühlen Fleck in einem Kessel mit kochendem Wasser.
	F	Il n'y a pas de coin frais dans un chaudron d'eau bouillante.
597	D	Selbst eine gute Sache ist nicht so gut wie nichts.
	F	Même une bonne chose n'est pas aussi bonne que rien.

599 D Lach nicht über mich, die betrunken auf dem Schlachtfeld liegt. Wie viele sind jemals aus dem Krieg zurückgekehrt?
F Ne ris pas de moi allongé ivre sur le champ de bataille. Combien sont revenus de la guerre ?

601 D Wie die Hand einer Person mitten in der Nacht, die hinter sich nach dem Kissen sucht.
F Comme la main d'une personne au milieu de la nuit cherchant derrière pour l'oreiller.

603 E In front, agate; behind pearls.
D Vorne Achat; hinten Perlen.
F Devant, de l'agate ; derrière, des perles.

605 E Hide the world within the world.
D Verstecke die Welt innerhalb der Welt.
F Cache le monde dans le monde.

607 D Vorbei! Die Jahre sind alle vorbei.
F Parties ! Ces années ont toutes été utilisées.

609 E Chew emptiness to pieces.
D Kaue die Leere in Stücke.
F Mâche le vide en morceaux.

611 D Nord, Süd, Ost, West haben keine Tür; die große Erde, Berge und Flüsse verbergen nichts.
F Nord, sud, est, ouest n'ont pas de porte ; la grande terre, montagnes et rivières ne cachent rien.

613–617 E Seven up and down, eight side to side.
D Sieben auf und ab, acht Seite zu Seite.
F Sept en haut et en bas, huit côte à côte.

619 E Receive everything as you would receive a single snowflake in your hand without fear.
D Empfange alles, so wie du eine einzelne Schneeflocke in deiner Hand empfangen würdest, ohne Angst.
F Reçois tout comme tu recevrais un seul flocon de neige dans ta main sans crainte.

621 D Welche Farbe hat der Wind? Woher kommt der Regen?
F Quelle est la couleur du vent ? D'où vient la pluie ?

623 D Nur dieser eine Gedanke.
F Juste cette pensée.

625 E Try to explain even one thing and you've already missed the mark.
D Versuche auch nur eine Sache zu erklären, und du hast bereits das Ziel verfehlt.
F Essaie d'expliquer ne serait-ce qu'une seule chose et tu as déjà manqué le point.

627 D Es ist wie das Zerschneiden eines Fadenbündels – ein Schnitt schneidet alle.
F C'est comme couper un paquet de fils – une coupe coupe tout.

629 D Donnerndes Schnarchen, Staub fliegt von den Balken.
F Ronflements tonitruants, la poussière vole des poutres.

631 E Ah yes! Quite obscure.
D Ah ja! Ziemlich obskur.
F Ah oui ! Tout à fait obscur.

633 D Manchmal sitzt du auf dem einsamen Berggipfel und lässt deine Hände in die belebte Kreuzung baumeln; manchmal döst du auf dem einsamen Berggipfel, während du auf der belebten Kreuzung bist.
F Parfois, tu es assise au sommet de la montagne solitaire et laisses tes mains pendre dans l'intersection animée ; parfois, alors que tu es dans l'intersection animée, tu t'assoupis sur le sommet de la montagne solitaire.

635–643 E Don't fantasize.
D Fantasiere nicht.
F Ne fantasme pas.

645 E Go and become the incense burner in the old shrine.
D Geh und werde zum Räuchergefäß im alten Schrein.
F Va devenir la brûleuse d'encens dans le vieux sanctuaire.

647 E Dead tree, cold ashes.
D Toter Baum, kalte Asche.
F Arbre mort, cendres froides.

649 D Verwechsle keine grüne Wolke mit einem gefärbten Phönix und hör auf, Weidenflaum für fliegenden Schnee zu halten.
F Ne confonds pas un nuage vert avec un phénix coloré, et arrête de prendre de la laine de saule pour de la neige volante.

PAGE CAPPING PHRASE

651 D Höre auf den Klang einer einzelnen Hand (die klatscht).
F Écoute le son d'une seule main (applaudissant).

653 D Was die Ähnlichkeit betrifft, ähnelt es sicherlich; aber was das Sein betrifft, ist es sicherlich nicht so.
F En ce qui concerne la ressemblance, cela ressemble certainement ; mais en ce qui concerne son existence, cela n'est certainement pas.

655 D Ihr Kopf ist lang – drei Fuß; seine Beine sind kurz – ein Zoll; sie schaut mich schweigend an, stehend auf einem Bein.
F Sa tête est longue – trois pieds ; ses jambes sont courtes – un pouce ; il me fait face en silence, debout sur une jambe.

657 D Unsere Sekte hat weder Wort noch Übermittlung; von hier aus sind es bis nach Indien achttausend Meilen.
F Notre secte n'a ni parole ni transmission ; d'ici, 770
la route vers l'Inde fait huit mille miles.

659 D Scheiß drauf, geh pissen.
F Va chier, va pisser.

661 D Gleichheit ohne Unterscheidung ist nicht die Buddha-Lehre – es ist schlechte Gleichheit. Unterscheidung ohne Gleichheit ist nicht die Buddha-Lehre – es ist schlechte Unterscheidung.
F L'égalité sans distinction n'est pas le Bouddha-dharma – c'est une mauvaise égalité. La distinction sans égalité n'est pas le Bouddha-dharma – c'est une mauvaise distinction.

663 D Halte eine Lampe brennend in einem dunklen Raum.
F Garde une lampe allumée dans une pièce sombre.

665 D Mit leeren Händen den Spaten ergreifen; während du zu Fuß gehst, reite auf dem Wasserbüffel; wenn eine Person über die Brücke geht, fließt die Brücke, das Wasser nicht.
F Les mains vides, saisis la pelle ; en marchant à pied, monte sur le buffle d'eau ; quand une personne marche sur le pont, le pont coule, l'eau ne le fait pas.

667, 669 E In the honey there's arsenic.
D Im Honig ist Arsen.
F Dans le miel, il y a de l'arsenic.

671 D Am dritten Tag geht sie in die Küche hinunter und wäscht ihre Hände, um den Eintopf zu machen. Sie hat den Essensgeschmack ihrer Schwiegermutter noch nicht gelernt und bittet ihre Schwägerin, das Aroma zu überprüfen.
F Le troisième jour, elle descend à la cuisine et se lave les mains pour faire le ragoût. Elle n'a pas encore appris le goût de sa belle-mère pour la nourriture et demande à sa belle-sœur de vérifier la saveur.

673 E As ignorant as a tub of lacquer.
D So unwissend wie eine Wanne voller Lack.
F Aussi ignorante qu'un pot de laque.

675 E The walls have ears.
D Die Wände haben Ohren.
F Les murs ont des oreilles.

677 E Little compassion obstructs great compassion.
D Ein bisschen Mitgefühl behindert großes Mitgefühl.
F Peu de compassion entrave la grande compassion.

679 E The pine tree, a thousand years of green.
D Die Kiefer, tausend Jahre grün.
F L'arbre de pin, mille ans de verdure.

681 D Die Sitzenden sehen die Stehenden, die Stehenden sehen die Sitzenden.
F Celles qui sont assises voient celles qui sont debout, celles qui sont debout voient celles qui sont assises.

683 D Im verlassenen Haus ist keine Person zu sehen. Das Schilf ist gebrochen, und wohin sind die Gänse gegangen?
F Dans la maison abandonnée, aucune personne n'est visible. Les roseaux sont brisés et où sont allées les oies ?

685 D Wie Wasser trinken und selbst heiß und kalt erkennen.
F Comme boire de l'eau et connaître soi-même le chaud et le froid.

687 D Hübsche Dame von Chao, bewegt vom Frühling, klettert auf den bemalten Pavillon. Mit nur einem Lied füllt ihre Stimme die Stadt mit Herbst.
F Jolie dame de Chao, remuée par le printemps, monte le pavillon peint. Avec juste une chanson, sa voix remplit la ville d'automne.

689 D Es ist zum Beispiel wie bei einem Brokat, der gewebt wird: Vorder- und Rückseite sind Blumen.
F Par exemple, c'est comme tisser du brocart : devant et derrière sont des fleurs.

691 D Wenn die Mutter hier ist, dann friert ein Kind; wenn die Mutter weg ist, werden nicht drei Kinder frieren?
F Si maman est là, alors un enfant a froid ; si maman est partie, est-ce que trois enfants n'auront pas froid ?

693 D Meine Frau schaukelt ihr Webgerät klack-klack,
Mein Baby spielt mit ihrem Mund ga-ga.
F Ma femme berce son métier à tisser clac-clac,
Mon bébé joue avec sa bouche ga-ga.

695 D Die Armut des letzten Jahres war nicht ganz Armut, aber die Armut dieses Jahres ist wirklich Armut.
F La pauvreté de l'année dernière n'était pas vraiment
de la pauvreté, mais la pauvreté de cette année est 772
vraiment de la pauvreté.

697 D Deine eigenen Nasenlöcher, die du bei der Geburt von deinen Eltern bekommen hast, sind in den Händen von jemand anderem.
F Tes propres narines reçues à la naissance de tes parents sont entre les mains de quelqu'un d'autre.

699 E No need to do it again.
D Es ist nicht nötig, es erneut zu tun.
F Pas besoin de le refaire.

701 D Sie sagt zu sich selbst: „Mein schönes Gesicht ist schwer zu übertreffen." Dann, als sie zum Kleiderständer kommt, zieht sie ein Gewand aus reiner Seide an.
F Elle se dit à elle-même : « Mon beau visage est difficile à égaler. » Puis, en venant au porte-vêtements, elle enfile une robe de pure soie.

703 E Make do with little.
D Komm mit wenig aus.
F Fais avec peu.

705 D Nicht wollend, dass ihr Gesicht mit Rouge und Puder verfärbt wird, bürstet sie leicht ihre „Mottenbrauen" und geht zu einer Audienz bei der Kaiserin.
F Ne voulant pas décolorer son visage avec du fard et de la poudre, elle effleure légèrement ses « sourcils de papillon » et va à une audience chez l'empereur.

PAGE CAPPING PHRASE

707 E Where the fish goes, the water is murky.
D Wo die Fische hingehen, ist das Wasser trüb.
F Là où va le poisson, l'eau est trouble.

709, 711 E Upset lakes overturn mountains.
D Aufgewühlte Seen stürzen Berge um.
F Les lacs perturbés renversent les montagnes.

713 D Wenn du ihre endlose Unzufriedenheit im Frühling sehen willst, es ist alles da, wenn ihre Nadel in Stille stehen bleibt.
F Si vous voulez voir son mécontentement sans fin au printemps, tout est là quand son aiguille s'arrête en silence.

715 D Das Himmelsfohlen rennt an einem Tag tausende von Meilen; hin und her, weit und breit, galoppiert es so schnell wie im Flug.
F Le poulain du ciel parcourt des milliers de miles en un 773
jour ; aller-retour, au loin, il galope aussi vite que volant.

717 D Leere Berge, keine Spur von meinem Kommen und Gehen. Eines Tages werden wir uns treffen – aber wo?
F Des montagnes vides, aucune trace de mon va-et-vient. Un autre jour, nous nous rencontrerons – mais où ?

719 D Die goldene Nadel hat nie ihre Spitze enthüllt, aber sie zieht den fadenlosen Jadefaden lang.
F L'aiguille en or n'a jamais révélé sa pointe, mais elle étire le fil de jade sans fil.

721 D Das nehmen, was auf dich zukommt, und weggehen.
F Accepter ce qui t'arrive et partir.

723 D Worte versagen.
F Les mots manquent.

725 D Der Löwe auf einem einzelnen Haar präsentiert sich auf einer Milliarde Haaren.
F Le lion sur un cheveu se montre sur un milliard de cheveux.

727 D Stelle deine Füße auf festen Boden.
F Mets tes pieds sur un sol solide.

729 E Already swallowed it.
D Schon geschluckt.
F Déjà avalé.

PAGE		CAPPING PHRASE
731, 733	E	Remote and free, not caught up in things.
	D	Fern und frei, nicht von Dingen gefangen.
	F	À distance et libre, pas pris dans les choses.
735	E	When alive your wealth is the dew on the grass; after death your fame is the flowers by the roadside.
	D	Wenn du lebst, ist dein Reichtum der Tau auf dem Gras; nach dem Tod sind die Blumen am Straßenrand dein Ruhm.
	F	Quand tu es vivant, ta richesse est la rosée sur l'herbe ; après la mort, ta renommée sont les fleurs au bord de la route.
737	D	Die Vernunft ist an ihren Grenzen, Gefühl und Intellekt vergessen – womit kann man das vergleichen?
	F	La raison est à ses limites, le sentiment et l'intellect oubliés – à quoi peut-on comparer cela ?
739, 741	E	Through the pure waves, there's no path. 774
	D	Durch die bloßen Wellen gibt es keinen Weg.
	F	À travers les vagues pures, il n'y a pas de chemin.

This book is published as part of the 8th edition (2023) of the Prix de la Société des Arts de Genève awarded to Bea Schlingelhoff and her exhibition, curated by Julien Fronsacq, at the Palais de l'Athénée from February, 29 to March 30, 2024.

Cet ouvrage est publié dans le cadre de la 8e édition (2023) du Prix de la Société des Arts de Genève décerné à Bea Schlingelhoff et son exposition, organisée par Julien Fronsacq, au Palais de l'Athénée du 29 février au 30 mars 2024.

Dieses Buch erscheint anlässlich der 8. Ausgabe (2023) des Prix de la Société des Arts de Genève, der an Bea Schlingelhoff verliehen wurde, und ihrer Ausstellung, kuratiert von Julien Fronsacq, im Palais de l'Athénée, 29. Februar bis 30. März 2024.

The Jury is made up of / Le Jury est composé de / Die Jury zusammen aus:
Julien Fronsacq (chairman/président/Vorsitz), Devrim Bayar, Giovanni Carmine, Justine Möckli, Mai-Thu Perret, Nina Zimmer.

This publication has received the generous support of the / Cette publication a bénéficié du soutien généreux de la / Diese Publikation wurde großzügig unterstützt von der Société des Arts, Genève.

Thank you: Devrim Bayar, Jean-Marc Brachard, Harry Burke, Giovanni Carmine, Samten Chödrön, Anna Chrusciel, Ligia Dias, Ed Fella, Julien Fronsacq, Gloria Hasnay, Yasemin Imre, Étienne Lachat, Nelson López, Justine Möckli, Mai-Thu Perret, Werner and Brigitte Schlingelhoff, Katharina Shafiei-Nasab, Lev Shoykhet, Alix Stria, Nina Zimmer.
Without them, this publication would not have been possible. Dedicated to the long life of MJKR.

Graphic Design:
Studio SMS (Katharina Shafiei-Nasab & Alix Stria)
Editors:
Julien Fronsacq, Bea Schlingelhoff
Translation & Proofreading:
Gudrun Werr, Julien Fronsacq, Bea Schlingelhoff
Proofreading Editor:
Émonie Fay Chetwin

Typeface:
PeggyKennett by Bea Schlingelhoff
Paper:
IBO Reflex (developed by Irma Boom) & Munken Pure
Print:
DZA Druckerei zu Altenburg

COLOPHON

Published by:
JRP|Editions
Rue des Bains, 39
1205 Geneva – Switzerland
www.jrp-editions.com

ISBN 978-3-03764-618-2
Printed in Europe

JRP|Editions publications are available
from the following distribution partners:

Switzerland
AVA Verlagsauslieferung AG
www.ava.ch

Germany and Austria
Publishers' Services Gabriele Kern
gabriele.kern@publisherssservices.de

France
Les presses du réel
www.lespressesdureel.com

UK and other European countries
Cornerhouse Publications, HOME
www.cornerhousepublications.org

USA, Canada, Asia, and Australia
ARTBOOK | D.A.P.
www.artbook.com

COLOPHON